American Legends: The Life of Johnny Carson

By Charles River Editors

Johnny Carson in 1970

About Charles River Editors

Charles River Editors provides superior editing and original writing services across the digital publishing industry, with the expertise to create digital content for publishers across a vast range of subject matter. In addition to providing original digital content for third party publishers, we also republish civilization's greatest literary works, bringing them to new generations of readers via ebooks.

Introduction

Johnny Carson (1925-2005)

"I know a man who gave up smoking, drinking, sex, and rich food. He was healthy right up to the day he killed himself." – Johnny Carson

A lot of ink has been spilled covering the lives of history's most influential figures, but how much of the forest is lost for the trees? In Charles River Editors' American Legends series, readers can get caught up to speed on the lives of America's most important men and women in the time it takes to finish a commute, while learning interesting facts long forgotten or never known.

Among America's comedians, few if any have had the kind of influence on pop culture and society like Johnny Carson, the iconic host of *The Tonight Show* from 1962-1992. In addition to winning too many awards to count, Carson is proof that imitation is the sincerest form of flattery, as admitted by subsequent comedy show hosts like Jay Leno and David Letterman, who not only vied to replace Carson but also used his format for their own shows (and still continue to do so).

Carson may have pioneered the format of *The Tonight Show*, but he had already been involved in comedy for decades before then, starting with performances as "The Great Carsoni" when he was still a teen. The magic shows and comedy continued into college, where he had a running gag about interviewing pigeons on rooftops and asking them about a local political controversy. Carson's work was hailed by comedians like Red Skelton, who invited him to become a writer for him, and Jack Benny, who invited him onto the show, all before he had turned 30.

For several years during the 1950s, Carson rotated around various daytime shows as host, meeting important friends like Ed McMahon along the way, but he made it big when he replaced Jack Paar as host of *The Tonight Show* in 1962. For the next 30 years, his mix of monologues, skits, and interviews would make his show must-see television on weekday nights, turning him into the highest paid television personality of the 1970s, and giving him the creative freedom to bring others along with him. In addition to bringing along his sidekick McMahon, Carson let guests host the show occasionally as well, thereby giving the spotlight to comedians like George Carlin, Letterman, Leno, and Joan Rivers. On the 25th anniversary of his debut on *The Tonight Show*, Carson earned a Peabody Award that labeled him "an American institution, a household word, the most widely quoted American."

American Legends: The Life of Johnny Carson examines the life and work of one of America's most important entertainment icons. Along with pictures of important people, places, and events, you will learn about *The Tonight Show*'s most famous host like never before, in no time at all.

Chapter 1: The Great Carsoni

"I was so naive as a kid I used to sneak behind the barn and do nothing." – Johnny Carson

John William Carson was born on October 23, 1925 into an All-American kind of family in Corning, Iowa. His father, Kit Carson (no relation to the famous cowboy), worked at the local power company, while his mother, Ruth, stayed home raising Johnny, his older brother Dick, and his younger sister Catherine. The Carson's moved several times during Johnny's early years before settling in Norfolk, Nebraska in 1933, and though America was in the throes of the Great Depression at the time, the Carson's did not feel the pinch as much as most families. Kit never lost his job, so even though they weren't wealthy, they also didn't have to wonder where their next meal was coming from.

That security ensured young Johnny had a normal childhood, and as a child, Johnny Carson was an unusual mixture of shy wallflower and class clown. However, the older he got, the more he enjoyed losing himself in another personality or in a performance, and he explained how he became comfortable making that kind of personality transition: "That's one of the things that goes against the grain of being brought up that you should be modest; you should be humble, you shouldn't draw attention to yourself. Well, to be an entertainer you gotta be a little gutsy, a little egotistical, so you have to pull back sometimes when people say, 'Well, he's stuck-up.' Stuck-up is only another word for self-conscious. You aren't stuck-up. You are aloof because you aren't very comfortable so you put up this barrier." He also noted, "There comes a time or a moment when you know in which direction you're going to go. I know it happened to me when I was quite young. I think it's when you find out that you can get in front of an audience and be in control. I think that probably happened in grade school, 5th or 6th grade, where I could get attention by being different, by getting up in front of an audience or even a groups of kids and calling the attention to myself by what I did or said or how I acted. And I said, 'Hey, I like that feeling.'"

When he was 12, Johnny's friend Phil McNeely showed him a catalog for magic tricks, and Johnny was fascinated, later recalling, "It showed exactly how [to do tricks] with a kit of stuff from some mail order magic house in Chicago. So I sent for it. I started making the things I needed and it was fascinating. I spent hours at it. Magic became my all-consuming interest." With magic, Johnny found a new way to relate to the world, and in time, it would give him both a social and financial future. His parents, however, thought it was merely a passing fancy, but while it was going on, his mother figured she should indulge him a little, so that Christmas, she gave him a beautiful black velvet banner embroidered with his new stage name: "The Great Carsoni".

From that time on, Johnny would perform for anyone he could get to watch. For a penny or two, any child in the neighborhood could be treated to the amazing feats of magic performed by their young neighbor, and as he got better, he added small parties and church socials to his venues. Carson would later recall, "I can't say I ever wanted to become an entertainer, I already was one, sort of—around our house, at school, doing my magic tricks, throwing my voice and doing the Popeye impersonations. People thought I was funny; so I kind of took entertaining for granted.... It was inevitable that I'd start giving little performances."

For young John Carson, performing helped him navigate the frightening waters of adolescence. He would remember his time in high school fondly, saying, "When I was a kid, I was shy. And I think I did that because it was a device to get attention. And to get that reaction is a strange feeling. It is a high that I don't think you can get from drugs. I don't think you could get it from anything else. The mind starts to do things that you didn't even realize it could do. I suppose it's the manipulation. I suppose it's the sense of power, the center of attention and the me-ism. And performers have to have that."

By the time Johnny was a senior in high school, his reputation for humor won him a place on his high school yearbook committee. As class historian, he took it upon himself to write a very humorous "last will and testament" for his high school's yearbook, the Milestone: "I, John Carson, being of sound mind and body (this statement is likely to be challenged by my draft board and the high school faculty)...can visualize 20 years from now when you sit by the radio (listening to Roosevelt)...you will say to your son—"I wish I could get hold of that #?$))&/ Milestone Staff."

Even at this young age, Carson displayed several hints of the style of humor that he would later make a part of America's late night experience. First, there was his self-deprecation, and Carson would build his career on the back of his own flaws. Also, there is the reference to Franklin Roosevelt, who was by this time well into his third term, a subject of both amusement and consternation for many in the nation. Finally, Carson pushed the envelope of what was then considered good taste with his discreetly veiled "profanity."

However, for Carson and most of his classmates, adolescence ended abruptly, because many high school graduates immediately had to enter the military. In fact, the thought was always with them, as Carson's reference to his draft board indicates. On June 8, 1943, just days after he graduated from high school, Carson entered officer training at Columbia University, and he later transferred to Millsaps College, where he continued to practice his magic tricks between drilling and learning how to shoot. By the time he received his commission as an ensign, the war was almost over, but he was still sent to the Pacific theater and assigned to the USS *Pennsylvania*. His initial work provided a rude awakening for the 19 year old, because a few weeks before he arrived, the *Pennsylvania* had been hit by a Japanese torpedo. According to Carson, "It practically blew off the stern and killed twenty guys. So she headed into dry dock at Guam. I was assigned to damage control, I guess maybe because I was the youngest officer and the most recently arrived. And my first assignment was to go down into that hole in the stern and supervise the bringing out of those twenty corpses and their personal effects. Jesus, that was an awful experience. They'd been down there eighteen days by that time, and I want to tell you, it was a terrible job."

Carson in the Navy

To keep fit and blow off some steam, Carson did some boxing while in the Navy, during which he had a perfect 10-0 record, quite a feat for someone who had never boxed before. However, he did not have long to pursue either his boxing or his naval career, because the atomic bombings of Hiroshima and Nagasaki brought the war to an end only a few months after he was commissioned. During the time between the end of the war and his own decommissioning, Carson worked in communications and decoding, which gave him plenty of time to practice his magic and a unique opportunity to perform for a very special person. Once, while delivering a decoded message, Carson recalled, "I walked in with this thing, and there was [Secretary of the Navy] Forrestal with the admiral, having breakfast. He asked me my name, and if I planned to stay in the Navy. I said 'No, sir,' and he asked what I wanted to do after I got out of the service. Well, I hadn't really given it much thought myself, but I had to say something. So I said I'd always been interested in being a magician and entertainer. Forrestal said, 'Can you show us some tricks?' And the admiral pulled out a deck of cards from somewhere. And there I was, after being up all night, at six or seven in the morning on Guam, doing card tricks for the admiral and the Secretary of the Navy."

Secretary Forrestal

Once he was back at home, Carson returned to college and enrolled in the University of Nebraska, where he pledged Phi Gamma Delta and made extra money by performing his magic act for various campus and fraternity events. By this time, he was charging $25 a show, which was plenty of money to afford hamburgers and nice clothes. Committed to performing and comedy, he devoted his senior thesis to an in-depth examination of Jack Benny's style of humor, and this thesis, along with his class work, earned him a Bachelor of Arts degree in radio and speech in 1949. At his parents' insistence that he have something practical to fall back on, he minored in physics.

Jack Benny

Chapter 2: Who Do You Trust?

"Talent alone won't make you a success. Neither will being in the right place at the right time, unless you are ready. The most important question is: 'Are you ready?'" – Johnny Carson

As was typical in the 1940s, especially with young veterans, Carson married just a few months after he graduated from college. He had met Joan Wolcott on campus in 1948, and the two began dating. She later explained, "Johnny was vulnerable and boyish. He was shy, but he covered it up with a very superior, scornful air that I sort of saw through. There were all sorts of fellows around saying I love you, all this and that. But I fell in love with John, who didn't do any of that stuff. I fell in love with the man that he was. I believed in him." Johnny and Joan were married the following year, and Joan soon became pregnant, with their first son Christopher being born in the fall of 1950. He was quickly followed by Cory, and then Richard.

Meanwhile, Johnny had gotten his first job at WOW radio and television in Omaha. Unlike his idols, Jack Benny and Bob Hope, Carson did not cut his teeth in radio but instead jumped straight into the new medium of television. His first show was a morning program called *The Squirrel's Nest*. He would later recall, "The trick was just finding something to do. We had turtle races, one of the more exciting things. There was no money in television in those days but nobody cared because you were learning what it was all about. We were all caught up in the idea that we were on television. You'd just go in and they'd kind of roll a camera out and you were on the air."

By far, Carson's most famous bit surrounded a local political controversy. The Douglas County Courthouse in Omaha was infested with pigeons, and the city council was determined to get rid of them. Of course, some people felt that the birds were a charming addition to the building and should be left alone. For his part, Carson remembered, "I simply took the pigeon's side. And I did a remote broadcast one morning. I got up on top of the building with a microphone. And I said, 'Just get me a record with some coos that sound like doves of pigeons.' So I went up and I asked the pigeons how they felt about this attempt to remove them. And then I would play the cooing and I would interpret what they said, that they were very saddened at the fact that the city government would try to move them off a public building. It got a lot of press and finally I think the Natural Gas Building or something like that offered to take the pigeons."

Another routine that Carson enjoyed no doubt influenced the eventual development of "Carnac the Magnificent." At that time, studios would receive pre-recorded tapes of celebrities answering questions that deejays were then expected to ask on the air, but Carson thought it was fun to change the questions. For instance, he was supposed to ask singer Patti Page when she began singing, but instead, he asked her when she began drinking, making her taped reply more hilarious than accurate: "When I was six, I used to get up at church socials, and do it."

With his experience in Omaha under his belt, Carson was ready for something bigger, so in 1951, he packed up his growing family and took a "vacation" to California. However, what he was really doing was looking for a new job, which he found at KNXT, a Los Angeles television stationed owned by CBS. His show was called *Carson's Cellar* because he claimed it was the "bargain basement" of comedy, but his biggest problem was that he needed a sponsor. After wooing prospective companies for months, Carson finally persuaded American Home Products to come on board, but the maker of anti-perspirants and depilatories was not a good match for Carson's humor. By 1953, the show was off the air.

Fortunately, Carson soon had an offer from another source, because famous comedian Red Skelton had seen *Carson's Cellar* and liked his style. He asked Carson write jokes and skits for his show. The following year, in 1954, Skelton was injured on the set and had to find a quick replacement to do the show that evening. He chose Carson, giving the young man his first national exposure. While this did not make an immediate difference in his career, it did plant seeds that would bear fruit well in the future, and Carson's name began to spread around the industry. One of the people that heard of Carson during this era was Jack Benny, who invited Carson to do a guest spot on his show. When Carson did a humorous job of imitating Benny and then claiming Benny was imitating him, Benny correctly predicted that Carson would soon find plenty of his own success as a comedian.

Red Skelton

Carson appearing on *The Jack Benny Show*

After Carson hosted a short lived game show called *Earn Your Vacation*, he had accrued enough name recognition that his next program was called *The Johnny Carson Show*. It premiered in 1955 and seemed destined for success, but the show was doomed to failure by an assortment of problems, as Carson remembered, "There were too many cooks telling me what to do and how to do it. There was no central control. The agency was putting people on without my knowledge, the scripts were being edited without telling me. I was sitting around like a dummy." As a result of these and other problems, the show only lasted just 39 weeks before being cancelled.

Disappointed with his time on the West Coast, Carson returned to New York City to look for more work, and he found it in 1957 as host of an afternoon game show called *Who Do You Trust?* The show had originally been called *Do Your Trust Your Wife?*, but the name was changed when Carson joined the show so that he could include unmarried guests. It was a big success, as each week featured new and well scripted interviews with average people from whom Carson would supposedly elicit surprising revelations. In many ways, it was one of the forerunners to the "reality shows" of the early 21st century, and it spawned similar gags with comedians interviewing people on the street, like Jay Leno's "Jaywalking" routine.

It is perhaps ironic that Carson was hosting a show about trust when he had so little of it in his personal life. By 1957, his marriage with Joan was on the rocks, but their marriage had always been plagued with problems from their earliest days. For one thing, the couple had radically different expectations about what married life should be like. Joan wanted a father at home each night, but while this was the image Johnny and Joan tried to portray to the public, especially during their many photo shoots for magazines, it was far from reality. In the real world, Carson believed that a man worked hard and long hours making a living, and that he was thus entitled to whatever type of fun he preferred, be it other women, drinking or just staying out all night with the guys. He did nothing to hide that he was often unfaithful from Joan; in fact, he was surprised that she even complained. When drunk enough and angry enough, he would lash out both verbally and physically, often leaving her with multiple bruises or a black eye.

For years, Joan kept their home life a secret, but the strain of living a lie began to take its toll, and she found herself needing someone to talk to. She began seeing a therapist and then other men. Perhaps she hoped that Carson himself would become jealous and that she would win him back, but he had little more interest in her fidelity than he did his own. He was fine with the status quo and didn't really care what she did, as long as she cared for the children and kept quiet about it. However, they couldn't go on as they were, and eventually, Joan insisted that Johnny move out in 1959. Carson would later say of the early days of their separation, "That's the lowest I've ever felt, the worst personal experience of my life. We'd been married ten years—since college, in fact. And children were involved—three sons. I think that's the worst guilt hang-up you can have, when children are involved. But divorce sometimes is the only answer. I think it's almost immoral to keep on with a marriage that's really bad. It just gets more and more rotten and vindictive, and everybody gets more and more hurt." Of course, that didn't stop him from cracking jokes about marriage, like, "Married men live longer than single men. But married men are a lot more willing to die." Or, "If variety is the spice of life, marriage is the big can of leftover Spam."

While Carson was losing one major relationship in his life, he was forming another. During his first year on *Who Do You Trust?*, he hired a new announcer named Ed McMahon, and McMahon quickly became the perfect match for Carson in both wit and quick thinking. Both men loved ad libbing, and McMahon proved to be one of the few that could keep up with Carson's sharp tongue. He was also satisfied with the number two slot and had no interest in trying to usurp his boss. Not only would McMahon become Carson's foil and business partner for the rest of his career, but he also became Carson's best friend. The two spent more time together off the set than they did on it, often finishing up their evenings in a nearby bar drinking into the early hours of the next morning.

McMahon

Unfortunately, while McMahon seemed to have a sense of self-control when it came to those late evenings, Carson was not as fortunate, and even he knew he had a problem. He would later recall, "We would go next door to Sardi's to have a small flagon of grape. And then we would come back to do a show at 6:30. And then we had one at 9:30 at night and I can remember coming in completely bagged. I'm not a good drinker, you know, two or three and I go bananas."

Indeed, before long, Carson's heavy drinking was affecting his performance on air, and his friends were concerned. They figured that since he was drinking more after his marriage ended, a new woman might help him cut back, and as a result, someone introduced him to Joanne Copeland. She worked at the studio as the hostess on *Video Village*, another afternoon game show they sponsored, but because living together would have caused too much scandal since Johnny was still technically married, Carson rented an apartment in her building the following year. They went places together and even took vacations with other couples, but they also argued and fought more than most couples. Still, they kept making up, even as Carson kept climbing the entertainment ladder.

Chapter 3: The Tonight Show

"New York is an exciting town where something is happening all the time, most unsolved." – Johnny Carson

In 1954, while Carson was writing for Red Skelton, comedian Steve Allen began hosting a late night program called *The Tonight Show*, and he all but created the genre of late night television, working without a script, hosting special guests and pulling crazy stunts as the situation demanded. Two years later, he left the show for something earlier in the evening, and Jack Paar took over for him. Paar was as high strung as Allen was relaxed, and soon Americans were making sure to watch the show every night just to see what was going to happen next.

By 1962, Paar was exhausted and ready to retire, and Carson was determined to replace him, even though he admittedly had little contact with Paar: "The only thing I can clearly remember…is that I met Jack in his office and said, 'Hi Jack!' I thought it was a very clever line. After all, I didn't want to overpower him. Beyond that I've had no dealings with him. I've never seen Jack Paar socially any place, and I was never a guest on the show when he was presiding. He might be an interesting guy to know. I just don't know. I really don't have the slightest idea what he's like."

Paar

Regardless, replacing Paar would make Carson the lord of the longest slot in television, almost

2 hours of air time every evening, but when he finally made his first appearance on the show, he opened to lackluster reviews. *The New York Herald Tribune* complained, "There was none of the free-wheeling frivolity, the titillating suggestive humor, the strong commentary, the boisterous what'll-he-do-next quality that so often sparked Paar's show. He is not the showman his predecessor was. But perhaps he will come along." Another critic, Jack Gould, was more optimistic, saying, "Mr. Carson's style is his own. He had the proverbial engaging smile and the quick mind essential to sustaining and season a marathon of banter...He began in an atmosphere mercifully free of impending crisis." The problem, of course, was that Carson had some huge shoes to fill. Jack Paar was an American institution, and even Carson's own mother was not sure he could do it, telling one reporter, "I thought it was interesting. I wasn't sure that John was the type for it. When Jack Paar had the show, it was more like an arena—so much controversy, all the time. John is a gentle, kind person. He's not controversial. But I think maybe he'll do all right."

Of course, the only people who really mattered were the viewing public, and they seemed more than ready to give Carson a chance. He carried around half of the viewing audience every night during his early months with the show, and those who tuned in watched with fascination as Carson introduced his own style to the show. For one thing, he used written scripts, right in front of him on his desk, rather than cue cards. While he had read and approved every word on them, the audience didn't know that, so if a joke didn't go over well, he tossed the paper aside as if he was just as surprised and disappointed as they were This bit of farce gave him a credibility with his viewers and made them like him even better. Moreover, as viewers got to know him, Carson also got to know his audience, saying, "You have to tailor your material to the medium. I can look at a piece of material and know fairly well whether it will play and be amusing. You have to learn to be an editor. You experiment sometimes. I'm sure Mel Brooks is not a comic who reaches the great percentage of the audience. He's kind of wild—but when he's good, he's near genius. I'll put him on the show. I'm much better with a Sam Levenson. He talks about kids and schools, and he won't offend. You just have to rely on your own judgment. If you do make a mistake, you'll find out soon enough—because suddenly you won't have an audience."

Carson also had a definite goal in mind when he took over *The Tonight Show*, as he would later explain, "I wanted the show to make the most of being the last area of television that the medium originally was supposed to be - live, immediate entertainment. I decided the best thing I could do was forget trying to do a lot of pre-planning. It all boiled down to just going out there and being my natural self and seeing what would happen."

On the first night that the show aired, there was a musical theme in the background. Written by Paul Anka and called "Johnny's Theme," it would become as much a part of the show as the band and the bad jokes. It would go on to open every program through Carson's last night in 1992. Another way in which Carson made the show his own was by bringing in McMahon to be his sidekick. McMahon would later recall:

"My role on the show never was strictly defined. I did what had to be done when it had to be done. I was there when he needed me, and when he didn't I moved down the couch and kept quiet. ... I did the audience warm-up, I did commercials, for a brief period I co-hosted the first fifteen minutes of the show..., and I performed in many sketches. On our thirteenth-anniversary show Johnny and I were talking at his desk and he said, 'Thirteen years is a long time.' He paused long enough for me to recognize my cue, so I asked, 'How long is it?' 'That's why you're here,' he said, probably summing up my primary role on the show perfectly... I had to support him, I had to help him get to the punch line, but while doing it I had to make it look as if I wasn't doing anything at all. The better I did it, the less it appeared as if I was doing it....If I was going to play second fiddle, I wanted to be the Heifetz of second fiddlers....The most difficult thing for me to learn how to do was just sit there with my mouth closed. Many nights I'd be listening to Johnny and in my mind I'd reach the same ad lib just as he said it. I'd have to bite my tongue not to say it out loud. I had to make sure I wasn't too funny—although critics who saw some of my other performances will claim I needn't have worried. If I got too many laughs, I wasn't doing my job; my job was to be part of a team that generated the laughs."

Before long, McMahon's opening phrase, "Heeeeeere's Johnny", had become part of the American lexicon, and Carson's show was also legendary for his opening monologues, because he was so committed to spontaneity that nobody ever knew what he was going to say. He explained, "It's always been a ritual with me. I don't show it to Freddie or Ed or anybody. If you don't show it to anybody, then you get fresh reactions." Of course, this meant that the monologue might not garner the kind of reaction he hoped for, so he had a backup plan. If the monologue got no laughs, the band would start playing "Tea for Two", and Carson would dance until the audience loosened up. Thankfully, most of the monologues were popular, and they typically ended with Carson doing a clubless golf swing toward the orchestra. Guest hosts would start to mimic that signature move by pretending to roll bowling balls stage left in place of Carson's golf swing.

Carson with McMahon and bandleader Skitch Henderson on New Year's Eve 1962

During the summer of 1963, Carson surprised his friends, and even perhaps himself, by deciding to remarry. He arranged for Joan to fly to Mexico and quickly formalize their divorce, so that there would be as little attention called to the matter as possible. Then he and Joanne planned a small wedding for August 17. Still, even after he had a new wife, Carson's first love remained his show, and as he grew to love it more, so did the people in show business.

One of the things that Carson brought to his show was a cast of dozens, all played by him. For example, one of these characters was "Honest Bernie Schlock", the host of the "Tea Time Movie", who would come on with his "Matinee Lady" and try to sell the audience a very unusual and useless product during long breaks between short segments of the fictional movie. Over the years, Schlock would be "replaced" by Ralph Willie and then Art Fern.

Then there was Carnac the Magnificent, a turban wearing mystic who would always be introduced by McMahon in the same way and then trip over the step up to the desk in a bumbling fashion. On one occasion, the desk was set up so that Carnac could actually fall through it and break the desk after tripping over the step. After implying that Carnac had been involved in some recent national or international disaster, McMahon would announce, "I hold in my hand the envelopes. As a child of four can plainly see, these envelopes have been hermetically sealed. They've been kept in a #2 mayonnaise jar on Funk and Wagnall's porch since noon today. No one knows the contents of these envelopes, but you, in your borderline divine and mystical way, will ascertain the answers having never before seen the questions."

Carnac would hold the envelope up to his forehead, come up with an answer, and then open it up to reveal a question that made the answer humorous:

"Billy Graham, Virginia Graham, and Lester Maddox" ... "Name two Grahams and a Cracker!"

"Over 105 in Los Angeles" ... "Under the Reagan plan, how old do you have to be to collect Social Security?"

"V-8" ... "What kind of social disease can you get from an octopus?"

"Debate" ... "What do you use to catch de fish?"

"Baja" ... "What sound does a sheep make when it laughs?'"

"Sis boom bah."..."Describe the sound made when a sheep explodes."

Soon, being on *The Tonight Show Starring Johnny Carson* was a rite of passage for any aspiring star, a sign that someone had made it to the big leagues. Many of today's biggest names in show business made their first major network appearances on *The Tonight Show*, like David Letterman, who would go on to have his own show and be a major competitor of Carson's replacement, Jay Leno. Standup comedian Jeff Foxworthy first introduced the country to Rednecks on an episode of *The Tonight Show*, and many comedians who got their first big break on Carson's show, including Jerry Seinfeld, Ellen DeGeneres, Tim Allen, Roseanne Barr and Drew Carey, went on to become television stars in their own right and have situational comedies built around their routines. In many ways, Johnny Carson filled in the space left after *The Ed Sullivan Show* ended in 1971.

Though Carson could be nasty to his own writers and as difficult to please as possible, he was typically kind to newcomers. One of these, Joan Rivers, later remembered her first time on the show, "He understood everything. He wanted it to work. He knew how to go with me and feed me and knew how to wait....He never cut off a punch line and when it came, he broke up. It was like telling it to your father—and your father is laughing, leaning way back and laughing, and you know he is going to laugh at the next one. And he did and he did and he did....At the end of the show he was wiping his eyes. He said, right on the air, 'God, you're funny. You're going to be a star.'"

On the other hand, one thing Carson wouldn't do was assist an interviewee by engaging in mock laughter. Canadian comedian Mort Sahl remembered what happened if an interview wasn't going well, "The producer crouches just off camera and holds up a card that says, 'Go to commercial.' So Carson goes to a commercial and the whole team rushes up to his desk to discuss what had gone wrong, like a pit stop at Le Mans."

However, people were willing to take their chances because appearances on *The Tonight Show* were good for publicity and business. In early 1966, Milton Bradley released a new game called Twister, and though children found it somewhat fun, the product was not selling well and was in danger of being pulled from the market. However, when Carson played the human pretzel game on the air with bombshell Eva Gabor, sales went through the roof, and Twister has been an important part of American culture ever since.

For his part, Carson enjoyed his success and the money that came with it, but he was also aware that he owed something to the world that had been so good to him. His Midwestern background had instilled in him the importance of giving back, as he told one reporter, "It's silly to have as one's sole object in life just making money, accumulating wealth. I work because I enjoy what I'm doing, and the fact that I make money at it-- big money--is a fine-and-dandy side fact. Money gives me just one big thing that's really important, and that's the freedom of not having to worry about money. I'm concerned about values--moral, ethical, human values--my own, other people's, the country's, the world's values. Having money now gives me the freedom to worry about the things that really matter."

Chapter 4: Staying On Top of Late Night Television

"By the simple law of survival, Carson is the best. He enchants the invalids and the insomniacs as well as the people who have to get up at dawn. He is the Valium and the Nembutal of a nation. No matter what kind of dead-asses are on the show, he has to make them funny and exciting. He has to be their nurse and their surgeon. He has no conceit. He does his work and he comes prepared. If he's talking to an author, he has read the book. Even his rehearsed routines sound improvised. He's the cream of middle-class elegance, yet he's not a mannequin. He has captivated the American bourgeoisie without ever offending the highbrows, and he has never said anything that wasn't liberal or progressive. Every night, in front of millions of people, he has to do the salto mortale. What's more, he does it without a net. No rewrites. No retakes. The jokes must work tonight." - Billy Wilder, 1978

Early on, Carson developed a formula that would keep the show popular for decades; he would take off every Monday and have a guest host fill in for him. The first of these hosts, Joey Bishop, would appear on *The Tonight Show* more than 175 times, and along with movie star Jerry Lewis, he would be Carson's "go to" guest host during the 1960s. Though Carson respected and appreciated these men, and the others that would sub for him through the years, he was not intimidated by them or worried about his own standing: "The ratings always sag when there's a replacement for a time. I think I do a hell of a better show...but I think I do a better show because I have an affinity for editing and pacing. I make comedians look as good as I possibly can. This show is a combination of a lot of things—music, comedy, talk—but you must have a personality around which the show revolves. The show depends on how he works with the acts, the way he performs; his attitudes and opinions are what carries this kind of show."

While Carson was happy to take center stage and talk about someone else, he did not enjoy talking about himself, but as he became more popular, he was besieged by more and more reporters wanting interviews. To put them off, he created a list of answers that they could use to answer any of their questions.

"1. Yes, I did.

2. Not a bit of truth in that rumor.

3. Only twice in my life, both times on Saturday.

4. I can do either, but I prefer the first.

5. No. Kumquats.

6. I can't answer that question.

7. Toads and tarantulas.

8. Turkestan, Denmark, Chile, and the Komandorskie Islands.

9. As often as possible, but I'm not very good at it yet. I need much more practice.

10. It happened to some old friends of mine, and it's a story I'll never forget."

While Carson was enjoying professional success, he was also happy on a personal level, as his second marriage seemed to be going well. He was under less pressure to succeed now, so he was able to spend his time as he liked instead of feeling like he had to see and be seen at all the best places. In talking about his evenings with Joanne, he told someone, "I don't like to go out much. We enjoy spending our time here, we have a comfortable home and we like each other's company. I'm not going to sit around in a roomful of people pretending to have a good time and saying, 'Oh, isn't this fun?' when it isn't. That's silly. People say, 'Oh, but you ought to get out—you ought to go to the movies or the theater more often.' Why? I think it's a waste of time, doing things you don't really want to because people thing you ought to."

However, in 1970, Carson met Joanna Holland at a time when his marriage to Joanne was on the rocks, having succumbed to the same combination of selfishness and infidelity that had killed his marriage to Joan. Though he was still married, he was happy to have Joanna become his mistress as long as she under stood the rules. According to one close friend, Carson's attitude toward the woman he was with was, "You're mine. You come when I call. If it's in the middle of the night, whenever. If I ever see your name in the paper, you're through. When I'm through with you, you get in the car and leave, except if I want you to stay overnight. And if I want you to stay overnight, you stay overnight."

Joanna Holland

Though she was a young, beautiful professional model with the world at her feet, these were the rules Joanna agreed to. Over the next two years, Carson would go through a very messy divorce and finally agree to pay Joanne a significant amount of alimony just to be free to marry Joanna. Then, during the party being held on September 30, 1972 to celebrate Carson's 10th anniversary with *The Tonight Show*, he announced that he had married Joanna. Of course, by this time everyone was talking about each of his wives' first names: Joan, Joanne and Joanna. When asked about this, Carson just quipped that it was an easy way to avoid having to buy new monogrammed towels.

Of course, so many short lived marriages elicited a certain amount of speculation, even in

Hollywood, but Carson was sanguine about it: "I couldn't care less what anybody says about me. I live my life, especially my personal life, strictly for myself. I feel that is my right, and anybody who disagrees with that, that's his business. Whatever you do, you're going to be criticized. I feel the one sensible thing you can do is try to live in a way that pleases you. If you don't hurt anybody else, what you do is your own business." All the while, he managed to keep cracking jokes about marriage: "My giving advice on marriage is like the captain of the Titanic giving lessons on navigation."

In 1972, Carson also agreed to move the taping of the show from New York City to Burbank, California, after several years resisting the idea because he preferred life on the East Coast. However, he eventually became disenchanted with the noise and crowds in New York, and unlike California, there were no nearby suburbs where he could live and commute to the studio. Thus, he chose to move to the West Coast with his new wife and the entire *Tonight Show* crew. When asked about his decision, he told reporters, "The main reason is the talent pool. There's not much television in New York anymore. When you do five shows every week for a year, it's a little sticky sometimes to find a large number of lively people in New York." As a result, Carson was soon introducing his show from 'beautiful downtown Burbank."

However, the move out west introduced a new set of problems for the show, and one that the producers could not have initially anticipated came up during the late 1970s. The crew filmed the show at 5:30 each evening for broadcast at 8:30 Pacific time (11:30 Eastern). They would transmit this live show via satellite to New York for editing, but the transmission was usually about two and a half hours long. Knowing that much of the show would be edited out, Carson and the members of the band would often make comments that were not suitable for public consumption, but some individuals began purchasing satellite dishes to catch programs being transmitted through the air. This allowed people to pick up *The Tonight Show* uncensored, and as word spread, people began setting their dishes to catch the often risqué show. As a result, NBC was forced to change to microwave transmissions during the early 1980s, and the studio eventually decided to simply move the editing facilities to Burbank.

Another problem arose in December 1973. Commenting on the many shortages plaguing the country at that time, Carson jokingly said that there was a threat of a severe shortage of toilet paper, but many of his viewers took his predictions seriously and rushed out to stock up on bath tissue. This in turn led to real shortages, and some companies had to ration supplies until they could make more, which created something of a self-fulfilling prophesy. Ultimately, Carson took a few moments from a January broadcast to apologize and clarify his comments.

The 1970s also introduced a new character to the show: Floyd R. Turbo, American. Played by a plaid coat wearing Carson, the character was meant to be "the epitome of the redneck ignoramus. I find the things (characteristics) each week when I go out to do...his gestures at the wrong time, his not knowing where he's supposed to be, his feeble attempts at humor, his talks about things he doesn't quite understand." He was known for such pithy observations as "If God didn't want us to hunt, He wouldn't have given us plaid shirts"; "I only kill in self-defense—what would you do if a rabbit pulled a knife on you?", and "Baseball the way it was meant to be played, on real grass, with no designated hitter and all white guys."

The late 1970s saw *The Tonight Show* win a number of awards, and for four years in a row, from 1976-79, it won a special Emmy for Outstanding Program and Individual Achievement. Carson was especially proud of the acclaim because he recognized the difficulty of maintaining such a high standard on a show that aired each weekday: "…a lot of the time TV is judged by the wrong standards. If Broadway comes up with two first-rate new plays in a season, the critics are delighted. That's a good season. But on TV they expect that every week. It's a very visible medium to jump on. And there's another thing that isn't generally realized. If you're selling hard goods—like soap or dog food—you simply can't afford to put on culture. Exxon, the Bank of America—organizations like that can afford to do it. But they aren't selling hard goods, and that's what the 'Tonight Show' has to do."

Politically, Carson was a liberal, but he also knew the danger of making his personal views known on his show, as he explained to *The New Yorker*, "Now, I think Hustler is tawdry, but I also think that if the First Amendment means what it says, then it protects Flynt as much as anyone else, and that includes the American Nazi movement. As far as I'm concerned, people should be allowed to read and see whatever they like, provided it doesn't injure others. If they want to read pornography until it comes out of their ears, then let them. But if I go on *The Tonight Show* and defend Hustler, the viewers are going to tag me as that guy who's into pornography. And that's going to hurt me as an entertainer, which is what I am."

For all that he enjoyed pushing the boundaries of good taste, Carson never forgot that those boundaries existed, and he was particularly hard on the supposedly avant garde humor of the 1970s: "It always amazes me, the things people regard as comedy in the theater. Any show where the biggest laugh is 'son-of-a-bitch' isn't much comedy in my book. I go to see what I think I'll enjoy. For me to spend three hours in a theater because something is charming just isn't what I want to do."

In 1979, Carson hosted the Academy Award Ceremony in Hollywood for the first time, and he hosted each of the following three years and again in 1984. In order to have more time for this and other extracurricular pursuits, Carson asked that *The Tonight Show* be cut to 60 minutes a show, and he also began using guest hosts even more often, making Joan Rivers his "permanent guest host" from 1983-1986. However, she subsequently left the show for her own talk show, *The Joan Rivers Show*, which aired on Fox opposite Carson's for the next season. Carson considered this a form of betrayal, and the two stopped being friends. Rivers would later recall that Carson wouldn't say a word to her when they bumped into each other, but either way, Jay Leno took over the Monday night slot in 1987.

Joan Rivers was not the only celebrity to have a falling out with Carson. Singer Wayne Newton often appeared on *The Tonight Show*, but during the mid-1980s, Carson began making jokes about him that Newton found offensive. After trying to contact Carson by phone, Newton finally showed up at the studio and demanded to see Carson. According to his recollection,

> "I said to Mr. Carson, I said, I don't know what friend of yours I've killed, I don't know what child of yours I've hurt, I don't know what food I've taken out of your mouth, but these jokes about me will stop and they'll stop now or I will kick your ass.

> He started to mumble, and I think he said something like, Wayne, I'm your biggest fan. I said, don't give me that crap. Don't give me that. I am here to straighten out whatever your problem is. And whichever way you want to straighten it out is fine with me.

> Johnny Carson was a mean-spirited human being. And there are people that he has hurt that people will never know about. And for some reason at some point, he decided to turn that kind of negative attention toward me. And I refused to have it."

While Johnny Carson was certainly hard to work with and live with, he was a very generous man when it came to good causes. In 1981, Carson established The John W. Carson Foundation to support causes related to the health and well-being of children. He was also very supportive of the financial needs in his hometown of Norfolk, Nebraska, donating much of the money needed to establish the Carson Cancer Center at Faith Regional Health Services and the Johnny Carson Theater at Norfolk Senior High School. He was also a significant contributor to the Elkhorn Valley Museum in Norfolk.

However, during this period, Carson also again found himself in divorce court when Joanna filed for divorce in 1983. Since California is a community property state, she would get 50% of all the assets Carson had gained during their marriage, which was no small issue, because Carson had spent much of that time being the highest paid person on television, making over $4 million a year. As a result, the proceedings dragged out, and the divorce was not finalized until 1985. Two years later Carson married Alexis Maas, and the fourth time turned out to be the charm, as their marriage lasted until Carson's death.

Understandably, this was a very difficult time in Carson's life, and he again fell into the habit of drinking more than he should. In 1982, he was stopped and arrested for driving under the influence of alcohol. His lawyer got the charge dropped to a misdemeanor, and Carson pleaded nolo contendere in return for a reduced sentence of three years' probation. As part of his sentence, Carson was only allowed to drive to and from the studio, and he was not allowed to have another person or even an animal in the car with him while he drove. He also had to take a class in understanding the effect of alcohol on driving.

As he got older, Carson became more and more interested in a hobby he had picked up in high school: astronomy. He owned several telescopes, including the famous Questar telescope, considered the best available at the time, and his star status allowed him to meet and even become friends with the famous astronomer Carl Sagan. In turn, Carson used his show to promote Sagan and his work, often inviting him to appear on *The Tonight Show*. Carson was one of the first celebrities to pick up on Sagan's unique speech pattern when talking about the night sky, and often mocked him by saying "BILLions and BILLions."

Sagan

Carson's other favorite hobby was tennis. He had always been athletic and found tennis to be a great way to keep in shape. When he learned that tennis legend John McEnroe was interested in buying his house in Malibu, he agreed to sell it to him only if he would give him six free tennis lessons. At first, McEnroe must have thought he was kidding, but Carson actually had the agreement written into the sales contract.

Chapter 5: Retirement

"Never continue in a job you don't enjoy. If you're happy in what you're doing, you'll like yourself, you'll have inner peace. And if you have that, along with physical health, you will have had more success than you could possibly have imagined." – Johnny Carson

In 1987, Carson celebrated his 25th year as the host of The Tonight Show. In recognition of this landmark, he received his own coveted Peabody Award from the Grady College of Journalism at the University of Georgia. In honoring him, the selection board observed that he had "become an American institution, a household word, the most widely quoted American…[so they] felt the time had come to recognize the contributions that Johnny has made to television, to humor, and to America."

However, a few years later, Johnny Carson suffered a tragedy that every parent fears most. On June 21, 1991, his youngest son, Richard, was killed in an automobile accident near Cayucos, California. Richard was an avid photographer and may have been trying to take some photographs of the scenic drive when he lost control of his car and drove off a steep hill. When Carson finally returned to work after Richard's death, he paid tribute to his son and his art by showing pictures of both as Stevie Ray Vaughan played "Riviera Paradise" in the background.

It is hard to say just how much Richard's death affected Carson's decision to retire from *The Tonight Show*, but either way, all good things must come to an end at some point. For *The Tonight Show Starring Johnny Carson*, that end came less than a year after Ricky's death on the evening of May 22, 1992. Though he was only 66 years old, Carson was understandably tired of the daily grind. During the opening monologue of his final episode, he told his audience, "If I could magically, somehow, that tape you just saw, make it run backwards. I would like to do the whole thing over again. It's been a hell of a lot of fun. As an entertainer, it has been the great experience of my life, and I cannot imagine finding something in television after I leave tonight that would give me as much joy and pleasure, and such a sense of exhilaration, as this show has given me. It's just hard to explain."

Then, after an hour long retrospective of his 30 years with the program, he closed with: "And so it has come to this: I, uh… am one of the lucky people in the world; I found something I always wanted to do and I have enjoyed every single minute of it. I want to thank the people who've shared this stage with me for thirty years. Mr. Ed McMahon, Mr. Doc Severinsen, and you people watching. I can only tell you that it has been an honor and a privilege to come into your homes all these years and entertain you. And I hope when I find something that I want to do and I think you would like and come back, that you'll be as gracious in inviting me into your home as you have been. I bid you a very heartfelt good night." The show then ended with one final image, a photo taken by Richard Carson himself. The following week, Jay Leno took over the show permanently from Carson.

Many people wondered how well Carson would survive without the stimulation of a daily show to tape; after all, George Axelrod had once observed of Carson, "Socially, he doesn't exist. The reason is that there are no television cameras in living rooms. If human beings had little red lights in the middle of their foreheads, Carson would be the greatest conversationalist on Earth." Even Carson himself left the door open for his return to television with some new show or project, but it would never happen.

As it turned out, Carson would take almost a completely opposite course. In the years following his retirement he was rarely seen on film and almost never sat for an interview. When NBC held their 75th Anniversary celebration, Carson even refused to participate. One of the few television "appearances" he made was when he voiced himself in a 1993 episode of *The Simpsons*, "Krusty Gets Kancelled." Carson also appeared on the TV Special *Bob Hope: The First 90 Years* that year.

Looking back on his career with *The Tonight Show*, Carson later recalled, "I'm often asked, 'What is your favorite moment during the 30 years you hosted [The Tonight Show]?' I really don't have just one. The times I enjoyed the most were the spontaneous, unplanned segments that just happened, like Ed Ames' infamous 'Tomahawk Toss' that produced one of the longest laughs in television history. When these lucky moments happen, you just go with them and enjoy the experience and high of the moment."

In November 1993 Carson called in to *Late Show with David Letterman* and even made a rare television appearance on the show in 1994. On May 13, Letterman announced that his sidekick Larry "Bud" Melman would be delivering the "Top Ten List" as Johnny Carson. Instead, Melman delivered the list badly and then stalked off the stage. Looking down, Letterman deadpanned that Melman had been given the wrong list and asked that the "real" list be used. At that moment, Carson himself came out as the band played "Johnny's Theme." The audience went wild, giving Carson a standing ovation, and the late night legend smiled and waved before asking Letterman if he could sit behind his desk. Letterman stepped aside, and Carson sat there for a short time as the crowd continued to cheer. Carson left the stage a few minutes later without ever reading the famous list, later claiming he had lost his voice due to a bad case of laryngitis. Whether or not this was true is anyone's guess, but Carson would never appear on television again.

Of course, Carson being on Letterman's show at all is a very strange turn of events, considering Letterman was the arch-rival of his replacement, Jay Leno. Just before Carson died, Letterman admitted that Carson would occasionally send him jokes that he would in turn work into his monologue, and upon his death, Letterman would mourn, "It's a sad day for his family and for the country. All of us who came after are pretenders. We will not see the likes of him again. He gave me a shot on his show and in doing so, he gave me a career. A night doesn't go by that I don't ask myself, 'What would Johnny have done?' He has been greatly missed since his retirement."

Although Carson worked hard to stay out of the limelight during his retirement, he still kept busy, primarily with charitable pursuits. In 2004, he donated $5.3 million to the University of

Nebraska Foundation, and the money was earmarked for the Department of Theater Arts at the University's Hixson-Lied College of Fine and Performing Arts. This donation was used to fund the Johnny Carson School of Theater and Film.

Chapter 6: Good Night

"I'd say it was quite important to let people hear the opinions of people like Paul Ehrlich, Carl Sagan, Gore Vidal, Margaret Mead. . . We've also taken an interest in local politics. One year, there were eleven candidates for Mayor of Burbank, and we had to give them all equal time. That was pretty public-spirited. But what's important? I think it's important to show ordinary people doing extraordinary things. Like we once had a Japanese guy from Cleveland who wanted to be a cop but he was too short, so his wife had been hanging him up every night by his heels. And it's important to help people live out their fantasies, like when I pitched to Mickey Mantle on the show, or when I played quarterback for the New York Jets." – Johnny Carson

Carson enjoyed the first few years of his retirement, living quietly at home with Alexis, playing a little tennis, and spending many evenings admiring the night sky. He had all the money and fame anyone could want and seemed content, but unfortunately, his happiness would not last. In the early morning hours of March 19, 1999, Carson woke suddenly in his home in Malibu to squeezing pains in his chest. Alarmed, Alexis called an ambulance and had him transported to the nearest hospital, where doctors diagnosed his complaint as a severe heart attack. Further tests showed multiple blockages in his heart, and within days, Carson had undergone quadruple-bypass surgery to open the blockages and repair as much heart damage as possible.

As the heart attack made clear, Carson's health was so bad due to his lifelong addiction to smoking. He had begun smoking as a young man, and he even smoked on the air during many of his early *Tonight Show* broadcasts. However, he began having problems with his lungs as early as the mid-1970s, and occasionally he even told people, "These things are killing me." Sadly he was right.

As the new millennium dawned, Carson was already developing symptoms of the lung disease emphysema that would eventually kill him. Soon he needed oxygen to help him breathe and regular treatments to try to clear his lungs. In the late summer of 2002, he admitted publicly that his doctors had told him he was dying, but he held on for more than two years. During the first few weeks of 2005, he was hospitalized at Cedars-Sinai Medical Center in West Hollywood in respiratory distress, and this time he would not get out alive, dying in the early morning hours of January 23, 2005. In keeping with the private way in which he preferred to live, there was no public funeral or memorial service. His body was cremated, and his ashes were returned to Alexis.

Of course, no one could stop the world from mourning in its own way. The sitting President of the United States, George W. Bush issued a statement praising Carson's good work both on and off the screen. *The Tonight Show with Jay Leno* hosted a retrospective and brought on many of Carson's closest friends and favorite guests, including Ed McMahon, Don Rickles and Drew Carey. Each took time to share what they remembered best about Carson, in between clips of the man himself giving monologues and harassing guests.

For his part, David Letterman paid tribute to the man who had given him his start by giving a monologue that he later admitted consisted entirely of jokes written by Carson himself. He brought on the former executive producer of *The Tonight Show*, Peter Lassally, as well as Carson's own bandleader, Doc Severinsen. In opening the show, Letterman observed that no matter what was going on in America or around the world, for thirty-years the viewing public had just wanted to be "tucked in by Johnny" at the end of their day. Severinsen closed the show with one of Carson's favorite songs, "Here's That Rainy Day."

Severinsen

When the cable network Comedy Central held its First Annual Comedy Awards Ceremony in 2011, one of the awards it gave out was the Johnny Carson Award. David Letterman was the first recipient of the prize, with Don Rickles winning it the following year.

Even after death, Carson kept on giving. He left $5 million to the University of Nebraska, and a few years later, his estate gave another million to the university to endow the "Johnny Carson

Opportunity Scholarship Fund." However, his biggest contribution was to his own John W. Carson Foundation; upon his death, they received $156 million from his estate, which made the foundation by far the largest charitable organization in Hollywood.

In 2012, PBS aired a two-hour documentary on Carson's life and career. Entitled *Johnny Carson: King of the Late Night*, it featured clips from the show and interviews with many who knew Carson best. One reviewer captured what the show portrayed, and really much of who Carson was, when he said, "If to know Carson was to find him unknowable, there nevertheless seems to be remarkable agreement among observers about who he was off-camera: smart, decent, loyal but also demanding loyalty, a person whose natural shyness was amplified by his Midwest roots…"

Bibliography

Bushkin, Henry (2013). Johnny Carson. Houghton, Mifflin,Harcourt.

Carson, Johnny (1965). Happiness is a Dry Martini. Doubleday and Company.

Carson, Johnny (1967). Misery is a blind date. Doubleday and Company.

Cox, Stephen (2002). Here's Johnny: Thirty Years of Americas Favorite Late Night Entertainer. Cumberland House Publishing.

De Cordova, Fred (1988). Johnny Came Lately. Simon & Schuster.

Ephron, Nora (1968). and now...Here's Johnny!. Avon Books.

Hise, James Van (1992). 40 Years at Night: the Story of the Tonight Show. Movie Publisher Services.

Leamer, Laurence (2005). King of the Night: The Life of Johnny Carson. Avon

McMahon, Ed (2005). Here's Johnny!: My Memories of Johnny Carson, The Tonight Show, and 46 Years of Friendship. Thomas Nelson.

Sweeney, Don (2005). Backstage at the Tonight Show, from Johnny Carson to Jay Leno. Taylor Trade Publishing.

Tennis, Craig (1980). Johnny Tonight: A Behind the Scenes Closeup of Johnny Carson & the Tonight Show. Pocket Books.